Winning by WORKING

Written by Cristie Reed

Content Consultant
Taylor K. Barton, LPC
School Counselor

Rourke
Educational Media

rourkeeducationalmedia.com

Scan for Related Titles
and Teacher Resources

www.rourkeeducationalmedia.com

PHOTO CREDITS: Cover: © Colleen Butler; page 4: © Emde; page 5: © jarenwicklund; page 6, 7: © kurhan; page 8, 9: © Library of Congress; page 10: © Beano5; page 11: © Yurilux; page 12: © Morgan Lane Studios; page 13: Mandy Godbehear; page 14: © kristian sekulic; page 15: © Ana Abejon; page 16: © Deborah Cheramie; page 17: Mauricio Jordan De Souza Coelho; page 19: © LifesizeImages; page 20: © kali9; page 21: © Spwidoff; page 22: © bzh22

Edited by Precious McKenzie

Cover and Interior Design by Tara Raymo

Library of Congress PCN Data

Winning by Working / Cristie Reed
(Social Skills)
ISBN 978-1-62169-909-5 (hard cover) (alk. paper)
ISBN 978-1-62169-804-3 (soft cover)
ISBN 978-1-62717-015-4 (e-Book)
Library of Congress Control Number: 2013937304

Rourke Educational Media
Printed in the United States of America,
North Mankato, Minnesota

Also Available as:

Educational Media

rourkeeducationalmedia.com

customersevice@rourkeeducationalmedia.com • PO Box 643328 Vero Beach, Florida 32964

TABLE OF CONTENTS

Work is Rewarding 4

Children's Work: Then and Now 8

Work At School and In the Community 14

Winning Work Habits 18

The Value of Work 22

Glossary 23

Index 24

Websites to Visit 24

About the Author 24

WORK IS REWARDING

Suppose you hear someone say, "There's lots of work to be done today. I'm going to need your help." How would you feel? Do you dread the idea of doing hard work? Or, do you think of work as a way to make an important **contribution** to your family?

Work is an important part of a well-rounded life. Work is done to take care of things we value. Work is done to make products, serve others, or as a contribution to the greater good.

When people experience the benefits of hard work, they learn that working hard is rewarding. Working hard creates a strong feeling of self-worth. Working hard gives you confidence and provides you with a feeling of success. Hard workers are winners!

7

CHILDREN'S WORK: THEN AND NOW

In pioneer times, children needed to work around the home. Boys had to do heavy chores such as farming, building, and clearing land. Girls had to cook, clean, do laundry, and care for their siblings. It was hard, but their efforts were necessary for the family's survival.

9

This vacuum cleaner doesn't even require anyone to be home to get the job done.

Family life has changed, but families still have lots of needs. Modern electronics and devices have made taking care of a home easier for everyone. Children no longer have to work to provide food and shelter for their family.

Make work fun

Listen to music.
Make it a game.
Work together.

Today, children have school work and extra activities that take up a lot of their time. Still, working and helping around the house is important to the overall **well-being** of every family. It takes all family members working together to build a safe and happy home.

Everyone can contribute to their home and family. Both boys and girls are capable of helping at home, even from an early age.

Make a chore chart

Keep track of chores that need to be done and use it as a checklist to track the chores that have been completed.

Inside Chores	Outside Chores
make beds	water plants
wash dishes	rake leaves
empty the dishwasher	clean windows
cook meals	mow the lawn
fold clothes	pull weeds
dust furniture	sweep sidewalks
sweep or vacuum floors	care for pets
clean room	trash and recycling
empty garbage cans	wash the car

WORK AT SCHOOL AND IN THE COMMUNITY

School is the first place that children learn about developing a strong **work ethic**. It is their first job. At school, children learn to become independent workers. They also learn to work cooperatively with others as part of a team or group. The adults at school, like teachers, counselors, and coaches are there to **motivate** us to learn.

But school work is really your work! You need to take ownership for your school work and homework. Both take a lot of **determination** and it's not easy. When students work hard at school, they are rewarded with a sense of **accomplishment**, good grades, and respect from their peers.

Successful schools and thriving communities are created by adults and children. Children can work to make valuable contributions to their schools and communities as **volunteers**. At school, older students can help younger ones as tutors or buddies.

Children can serve their community as part of a team or work group. Work alongside others to complete big projects that benefit everyone.

WINNING WORK HABITS

Being a successful worker means practicing a few good habits. Try out these habits to help you with work at home, school, and in the community.

1. *Get motivated*. Think about the importance of the job.
2. *Be **persistent** and don't quit*. Keep trying until the task is complete.
3. *Use determination*. Set a goal and work to reach that goal.
4. *Be **resourceful***. Find ways to make work easier or more fun.
5. *Be **conscientious***. Try to do your best on every task.
6. *Learn how to handle stress*. If a task is difficult, step back and ask for help.

Get Ahead with Hard Work

Tasks get completed quicker and you have more time for other activities.

Working hard gives you a sense of accomplishment and helps others at the same time.

Work with adults to learn winning work habits. Talk to parents and teachers to learn about their experiences with work. Adults can share their successes and their challenges. You can follow the examples of successful adults and learn how to handle important responsibilities.

Adults can help kids develop a strong work ethic.

THE VALUE OF WORK

Work serves a purpose. People must work to achieve their goals in life. As people grow up, they learn how to take care of themselves, their family, friends, and possessions. Positive feelings come from a job well done. Working hard inspires people around you to do the same. Learning to work hard prepares you for the future. Hard work is essential to becoming an independent and successful adult.

GLOSSARY

accomplishment (uh-KOM-plish-muhnt): something done successfully

conscientious (kon-shee-EN-shuhss): making sure you do things well and thoroughly

contribution (kon-truh-BYOO-shun): giving money or help to a person or organization

determination (di-tur-mi-NAY-shun): to act with a firm purpose

motivate (MOH-tuh-vate): to encourage someone to do something

persistent (per-SIS-tuhnt): continue without being discouraged

resourceful (ri-SORSS-fuhl): good at knowing what to do or where to get help in any situation

volunteers (vol-uhn-TIHRS): people who do a job without pay

well-being (WEL-BEE-ing): health and happiness

work ethic (werk ETH-ik): a belief in the importance of work

INDEX

benefits 7

chores 8, 13

community 17, 18

contribution(s) 4, 6, 16

family 4, 8, 10, 11, 12

habits 18, 20

school(s) 11, 14, 15, 16, 18

successful 16, 18, 20

well-being 11

work ethic 14, 21

WEBSITES TO VISIT

www.knowitall.org/kidswork

www.kids.usa.gov/jobs/index.shtml

www.theleaderinme.org/the-7-habits-for-kids

ABOUT THE AUTHOR

Cristie Reed lives in Florida with her husband and her dog, Rocky. She has been a teacher and reading specialist for 32 years. When she was a child, her mom and dad taught her to have a strong work ethic. She wants children to know that you can achieve your dreams through hard work in school and in life.

Meet The Author!
www.meetREMauthors.com